DIALOGUE FOF

JILL WALLIS

THE LITTORAL PRESS

First Published 2005

The Littoral Press
10 Prail Court, Vesta Close
Coggeshall, Essex CO6 1QG

© Jill Wallis 2005

The right of Jill Wallis to be identified as author
Of this work has been asserted by her under
The Copyright Designs and Patents act 1988

British Library Cataloguing-in-Publication Data:
A catalogue record of this book is available from
The British Library

ISBN 09541844 –9-1

Printed by 4edge Ltd. Hockley, Essex.

2

FOREWORD

My husband Chris and I had reached a very sunny place in our lives. We had jobs we liked, our children were happy and successful and we were completely sure of our love for each other. I remember the conversation we had, congratulating ourselves on our good fortune, and celebrating the prospect of all the good years to come. A few weeks after that conversation I came home from work to find Chris having an epileptic seizure, and our lives changed forever.

Chris was energetic, witty, charismatic and talented. He filled any room he entered. For all who knew him it was almost impossible to accept that a man like this could succumb to cancer and die at 48. The day his brain tumour was diagnosed, I began a diary – something I'd never done before. In it I poured out my true feelings, while trying to be as positive and cheerful as I could for him and our families. From the day he died, I stopped being able to write in it. For six months I struggled on, writing nothing, until finally I knew I had to exorcise some of the events and feelings which were haunting me. Thus began this collection.

Chris's tumour was located in the language centre of his brain, which meant that this articulate and intelligent man slowly lost the ability to speak, and, near the end, to understand speech. It meant was that we couldn't have the conversations I at least longed to have as the end of our life together grew near. Later, as these poems emerged, I realised that all of them were addressed to him, as I tried to tell him the things I hadn't been able to in his life.

One of the hardest things when someone you love dies is the sense of betrayal you feel in trying to rebuild your life without them. At my lowest ebb I explained to my brother that I couldn't bear the thought of leaving Chris behind. His reply was 'You aren't leaving him behind, you're going ahead to find the path and when you've found it, you will go back for him.'

Chris, here I am. In these poems I've finally come back for you.

To Chris, of course
Loved life
Loved laughter
Loved

CONTENTS:

OWL PELLETS

When owls consume their prey,
they swallow tiny creatures whole,
bones, feathers, fur, entire.
And later,
all that's good extracted,
eject a smooth-skinned pellet,
a hoard
of tiny bones, wrapped in their own hide;
a neat encapsulation of the small life lost.

My poems are like this;
each one a memory which,
when I first lived it,
was also swallowed whole,
no time to taste it or digest,
as, one upon another,
such a feast of griefs I bolted.

But long months later I revisit them,
finding myself in pain anew,
from shards lodged deep within my gut.
And so I wrap each flesh-stripped skeleton in words,
regurgitate it,
on the waiting page,
licked smooth now by language.
This somehow spares my tender core from further wounds.

I leave it there for others to dissect,
to find the story of the death within,
for I have done with it.

SEIZED

Bolt upright in the chair
I found you,
head back,
eyes open,
though gazing
into empty air.

Just for a moment
I thought –
a joke?
I spoke your name
once half-laughing,
once, urgently,
in fear.

Suddenly
your body answered.
A juddering seized you.
From waist to head
like a toy in a spiteful grip
you jerked,
your face the colour of a three-day bruise,
soundless,
as you listened,
to the inner music
of this dance macabre.

Meanwhile,
I stammered out my summons
to a stranger.

As your possessor loosed its grip,
I heard the ambulance,
its growing wail
an echo of my grief,
turned back to see
two great tears

roll down your livid cheeks,
your knees,
in some perverted genuflection,
lift to your chest
and fall back.

As the wail grew louder
inside my head and out,
I thought
as clearly as if spoken,

nothing
will ever be the same
again.

NO RETURN

With outward calm we packed the little suitcase,
as if preparing for a weekend trip,
slippers, razor, simple homely things.
We set the breakfast table,
dry-mouthed, smiling,
each masking what we felt
to ease the other's fear.
Just one more trip into the lair of medicine,
another visit to the alien world,
which over months had dealt such cruel blows.

But this time I would have to leave you,
to tear our fear in half and leave you there with yours,
while, clutching mine,
I drove back home alone.
Tomorrow they would open up your skull,
and put your mind and memories
to the knife,
to excise the intruder
squatting in your brain.

We drove the journey, mostly silent,
each one absorbed in holding down the swell
of fear and love and utter horror.
I parked the car,
first taste for me of what became a ritual,
and climbed into the waiting city bus.
'Two to the infirmary,' I asked the driver,
'and one return.'

And in those words,
though spoken to a stranger,
I see now I was saying my first
goodbye.

PARALLEL UNIVERSE

They ask if I will leave your bedside for a moment,
come to see the doctor in her room.
'I'm really very sorry,' says the doctor,
and truly I do see pity in her face,
'I need to talk to you about resuscitation.'

I close my eyes.

Nine months ago we flew to Barcelona.
you ordered us two coffees in Catalan
as we sat,
sated with Gaudi,
in the sun.
But here today
they ask if they should let you die,
should one more seizure like the two this morning,
set off a stroke which cascades through your brain,
washing away your consciousness,
or what remains.

I ponder syllogisms,
ones my Logic training left untutored:
if A then B, if C then D.
If all you're doing is swallowing your tongue,
and might recover,   .
I've asked them please to rescue you again.
But if the blood,
a cerebral tsunami,
has erased you,
I think perhaps it's best to let you go.
Does that seem fair?
The doctor nods,
that's very clear,
and leaves to write my verdict in your notes.

I close my eyes

I see you smiling at me, over Spanish coffee.
A tear escapes. I let it slide.
Then dry it,
and return to your bedside.

TIDES

You gaze, unblinking, mildly, at me,
your face a smoothed sheet,
youthful
as if your life has bled like molten wax,
sliding from those doll-like pupils
downward,
smoothing every mark of memory
to blankness.

Marooned upon your inner raft you float,
ebbing and flowing,
tugged by the siren tumour-tide,
closer, sometimes,
so I nearly have you,
stretching for me,
here on shifting sands,
then further,
till your distant signals
barely reach me through the banks of fog.

And with each tide that turns, I ask,
though silent,
Is it now that I must speak?
For if I wait for your returning
this next may be the one
that takes you
over the horizon
of that inner sea,
and all chance lost to me forever
to say to you,
for whom all words are riddles,
the only one
that's left to me to say.

Goodbye.

LAST NIGHT

The end was near
and so I spent the night beside you in the chair,
for fear that you would leave me softly in the darkness
while I slept on,
or wake from that deep well you lay in,
one final time,
and I not be there
to glimpse a last connection in your eyes.

You did not waken,
though at times your eyes would open and I'd speak your name,
but you were gone from me already.
And, some time in the darkest, stillest hours,
I took your hand and held it, warm, against my breast.
All that long night I held it there,
your skin and mine as they belonged,
together,
till morning came.

DUST TO DUST

I cannot scatter the ashes,
this one coherence left to me of you.
To plunder handfuls of your body,
even this,
this bone-fragmented, fire-leached dust,
of living flesh,
I cannot
can
not
scatter.

Masked against your bone-dust,
I pour you through this plastic funnel
into the deep vase.
But as I pour,
and watch you sucked into the shadowed depths,
stealthily comes a soft breath,
exhaled from the vase's mouth.
It curls and spirals,
ectoplasmic, ghostly.
Creeping round the funnel's tip
it slides into the empty air.
Like a genie loosed,
this smoke of you dispels,

and deeply, deeply,
as the mask slips,
I breathe you in.

ELEPHANT

The elephant in the room,
I've heard it called,
where some enormous fact
is just ignored,
and those who share the room
avert their gaze,
or talk across it brightly,
rictus-smiled.

And so it was
when you came home to die.
We all could see – and talk of – death's grim props,
of wheelchairs and commodes
we spoke at will.
Paralysis, aphasia, all named,
and when you slipped into a silent world,
we ensured the cheerful chatter still prevailed,
sympathised with every minor loss,
tutted over hair fall, treated squints,
to ease burned skin we rubbed in cream.

But of your life we never spoke a word.
And so the elephant of loss that stalked the room
remained.
And you,
your death unspoken,
stole away.

BURGLARY

While you lay dying, our home was burgled.
The outer damage slight,
no squalid mess,
but I was charged to list our losses,
carefully, with values named and proved.

Some items came to mind at once as missing;
your watch, my ring, our camera.
For some I had an old receipt,
could put a price upon their heads.

The Dubai watch you bought, with such delight
at last with cash enough to treat yourself,
the watch your son would wear with pride today,
but sadly they don't make that model any more.
They gave me cash.

The ring you bought me when we first began,
not dear at all, but dearer still than gold.
Of course I could replace it with a match,
but what would be the point?
They gave me cash.

The camera, (with pictures in it of your final scars)
which took each image that I have of you,
they gave me cash.
I bought another.
It's still unwrapped.

But some things that were stolen weren't noticed,
till much later,
when I next needed them.
Each time a stab, another sharp reminder
of losses yet to be uncovered.

While there was cost financial in these losses
this was refunded.
But those of 'sentimental value',
that saccharine, demeaning name for things
you cannot place a value on,
and thus
are priceless,

they have not been replaced,
nor can be, ever.

That's what I found when I was burgled.
And what I found too, later,
when you died.

MARRIAGE VOWS

With all your worldly goods,
you once endowed me,
(along with body-worshipping, which then seemed more the prize).
I thought it meant your terrible LP collection
your bits of timber and your ancient drill
the full-size cardboard statue of Rick Wakemen
those old bell-bottoms and your platform shoes.

I didn't think that it might come to mean
your memory,
your mind
and all that helps a man to be.
I didn't realise you'd hand your life to me
and ask me
to weigh up what you should do.

You said you knew you could no longer understand
what doctors said,
or what the options were,
could not remember even
what disease you had,
what each pill was for
and when to take it.

You said you trusted me to do these things,
to make decisions
which would risk your life.
To tell them they could cut you,
hurt you,
frighten you,
remove your mind in chunks
and fry your brain.
You said you'd trust me always
to look after you,
to make the choices
you yourself would make.

I knew that you had given me
a precious thing,
when, years ago,
you gave yourself to me.
I thought we were exchanging life
for loving life,
but now I see that it was not an equal gift.
You gave me your life much more fully that I ever dreamed
but what I then repaid you with
was death.

GRAND CANYON

We gazed in speechless wonder
from the rim,
aghast at this astounding cosmic wound,
its totally non-human scale,
while heat reflected upwards
like a blow.

I always knew that one day I'd return,
unable to absorb it at one sight,
but this was not the context I'd foreseen.

For though I gaze again,
my hand in yours,
at devastation too vast to absorb,
this time there's no retreat from its embrace.
This time I must descend into the deep.

I knew of course the journey grief would be,
one taken through a brutal hostile land,
so steep the path zigzags
like razor-slash,
a hundred yards of toil
for each foot gained.
The only ones who get through
are the laden,
who must carry all their water
on their backs.

And this is what I see now
is my journey.
To struggle down
into this desperate place
for which,
with love alone,
I'm weighted,
to ease the parching agonies of grief.

And even if I make it to the bottom,
the other side awaits
my upward climb.

For days, then weeks, I stood there,
unable to accept
the trial ahead.
But when I baulked
it wasn't at the journey
or any of the gruelling times to come.

What froze me was the cruel realisation
that you must stay
behind me on the rim.

When you left me,
no other choice was offered,
but I am free to hold you close
and stay.
Yet all my future lies
across that canyon,
so, somehow, I must reach the other side.

Until I do
there can be no acceptance,
no chance of life restarted or rebuilt.

But oh the painful shame
of this betrayal.

To tear my eyes from yours
and turn my back,
to leave you ever stranded
and discarded,
till,
in the heat-haze fading,
you are gone.

LOST PROPERTY

So, what was lost?
I'll make out an inventory,
so I can claim,
know what I must replace.
In categories, yes,
that's best for order,
and to guard against omissions.

So, what is lost?

Our past –
a large collection this -
the memories of all we shared,
of love, of laughter,
pain and healing,
fear and comfort,
all the things you were to me,
my whole life's engine,
sparkling wit, biting scorn,
gentle warmth,
passion, challenge, need and trust.

Of course I have my memories of you
but who now has your ones of me?
Of who and what and how I was
when I was Chris's wife?

That's what is lost.

So to my present -
a sharper loss this -
your voice, your kiss,
your body in my bed;
your smile, your smell,
your skin under my hand;

your need for me,
love of me,
joy in me;

your plans, ideas,
making, doing, being;
driving both our lives
and building both our dreams.
Your eyes,
in which I saw myself
reflected,
which told me who I am.
Your love,
the only thing which now could bring me comfort,
that's what is lost.

Then to my future -
the biggest, deepest
and most precious loss -
Our hopes and plans,
a world to see
together,
grandchildren we would meet
and all our family's joys.
More endless layers
of love and knowing
to unfold,
careers and conquests, sports and passions,
exotic dreams and daily pleasures,
squeezing out the juice of all life's fruits,
in wondrous recipes
you'd lay upon my table.

I've lost the sun
that nourished me to grow,
I've lost the man
I'd only partly come
to know

and planned to spend
my life exploring.
Who knew my deepest places
and who found me good.
I've lost my shadow, my reflection
and my maker.
Like a jewel
which needs the light to make it sparkle,
I am forever now
bedimmed.

So I have listed, partly,
what was stolen.
Yet still I know my claim
cannot be met.
A property which has such
private value,
can never,
new for old,
be recompensed.

AGE GAP

For six months of the year
I'm four years older.
Then round comes my birthday
and makes it five.

I never used to like that date-click forward,
but much preferred your birthday's reverse shift.
It's not as if the age-gap really mattered,
yet still each year your birthday
made it better,
closing up the gap,
however small.

But suddenly this year
your day made no impression,
I held my place,
my five years lead on you.
A fact I didn't see until this moment,
as my birthday comes upon me.

This week I move away again, as always,
except, this time,
the date clock clicks to six.
And now another consequence
is shown me of death,
which fixes you in time,
as I grow old.
Thus every year the gap between
will widen,
until,
quite soon,
I'll have to face the truth.

I'll be too old
to love a man
as young as you.

LEVELS

I'm sinking now,
to another level;
a deeper pit,
with a wider vista,
though shrouded in shadow;
an outer purgatory
or an inner journey.

I stare at the big truths,
from which, before,
my gaze was kept averted -
blinded by my tears -
and they stare back, impassive.

What is it that I have
and you have not?
Have you anything,
or anywhere?
I cannot even frame the questions.
Do I speak of time, or place,
of matter or of mind?
-I have no credulity for souls-
for I have no sense of you,
no presence,
and,
equally a lack,
no absence.
More a life
which isn't you,
than a life
in which you aren't.
For not to be here
implies that you are there,
that there is a you to be absent
and a there for you to be.

But you are in a freeze-frame,
rather than one empty.
It's we who move away,
go forward,
on,
while you remain,
like an insect in a tomb of amber
held forever in your life-like, frozen pose,

suspended.

DO THE MATHS

I find, whenever,
in this world
which will insist on going on,
I read of someone's death,
and given age
my brain, unbidden,
does the maths.
Along a neural pathway long worn smooth,
subtracting, synapse-sharply,
forty-eight,
the age you were,
will always be.

I calculate at once
how many extra years,
this stranger had
that you did not,
and grudge them.

Odder still is how those years
the years that you and I,
had you been this dead stranger,
would still have left to plunder,
seem so much longer,
now they won't be lived,
than they once did, when,
unknowing of your fate,
we counted our inheritance.

Like miser's gold,
which in my grasp
had never seemed enough,
it now seems,
now that all is stolen,

a priceless hoard.

SKYDIVE

I crave a victory;
a challenge with an outcome,
with an end.

Each day I take another step
along an endless path
that stretches on to the horizon,
without relief.

And what would be success in this cruel fight?
To learn to lose you
and to live without?
What prize is that?

And so I struggle on,
my only triumph that I move at all.
For where I reach is only mirror-image
of my starting-point.

Upon a windswept moor,
one standing-place is much like any another,
all bleak, all barren.

And so I seek a different challenge.
I search for battles I can win,
a sharper, closer, finite fear,
to focus all my black internal thoughts.

I choose a pointless danger;
to hurl myself in terror from a plane.
Not for triumph, or for glory,
not even for the pittance I will raise.

I do it so that I may have a different pain,
another fear, which, though intense
and close to being beyond my strength,
will end.

SEEING SINGLE

I have to learn to live again in the world,
to see it once more
through my own eyes.
For now I see
what you would see,
believed you'd see,
but cannot.
Thus each view is seen
through a distorting lens
of pain, loss,
guilt that I can see
and you cannot.

It's cruel for me to gaze on sights
you would have sought,
and I come to understand
that, every time we
looked at life together,
I looked with double gaze,

and now must teach my spliced self
to refocus.

In seeing single
I must see for me alone.
I cannot use you any more
as my viewfinder,
but must start to scan
my own horizons
and so learn
to frame the world
from my perspective,
without your shadow falling over me.

Once I've learned to know the world like this,
perhaps I will be freed
from seeing life through you,
to seeing it for you.

As a gift from me,
from the sighted
to the blind.

OPTIONS

It's not that I intend to die.
I'm not planning it or choosing methods,
not hoarding pills or sharpening razors,
no need just yet to confiscate my laces.
It's just becoming harder to intend to live.

Because I'm getting clearer what that life will be,
and it's not enough.

I know I'm lucky, count my blessings,
home and job,
friends and health,
those who love me,
even some who need me,
but it's not enough.
Not even close.

It's not just what I've lost.
It's that the things I haven't lost
are cheapened.
While they were secondary,
they were joyful
but on their own,
they're not enough.
The icing on the cake can only be
if you have a cake.

I can't promote the chorus
to a starring role,
expand them so they fill a life.
Not one that's stretched
to take in you.
Like a diet winner
swamped by pre-loss clothes,
I feel the empty fabric of my life
balloon around me.

And so it is I think about my death.
Not dying - I have no appetite for that -
but being dead.

For I don't know if there can be
another life.
And even if there could,
that's not so different
from contemplating death,
involving as it does
such utter reconstruction
of what I saw my life to be.

Maybe to be dead is simpler?

Strange that going on being
takes more adjustment,
than just not being at all.

EMBROIDERY

A friend has an embroidered verse
Upon her bathroom wall,
It says we must not judge god's plan,
Until we've seen it all.

It claims this plan's a tapestry
Which, till it's all complete,
Cannot reveal the true effect
Of every thread discrete.

It says the threads of purest black
Which represent our grief,
Will only then be understood
For now we trust belief.

It claims these threads will then be seen,
To have their vital place,
To make explicit god's intent,
Revealing his true grace.

What I believe is that a plan
Which, so it can be seen,
Requires such grief and loss as this,
Is frankly quite obscene.

WHO'S COUNTING?

Mathematics rules the world,
some great thinkers say.
A big claim
beyond the reach of lesser minds.

But now I see,
beneath the seeming alchemy of love,
deeper patterns do lie.

For love can effortlessly multiply
each single joy
and make it double,
for being shared.

Each pain,
from irritation,
to unutterable loss,
is somehow halved
by resting it a moment
in a lover's heart.

But if love dies,
then all the cold numerical
malice
of a mathematical world
is suddenly uncovered.

On an exponential
Richter scale
of loss,
negative and positive attract
the same magnification.
Each joy divided
almost to nothing,
when felt alone,
each grief multiplied
to the nth degree.

In this binary world
where all can be reversed,
in sudden tessellation across life's axis,
when prime number one
is switched
to absolute
zero.

IT'S NOT A COMPETITION

Around me, as the family now absorbs
the loss of father, brother, son,
I see a strange disturbing process build,
a system of equivalence,
a hierarchy of distress defined.

Sisters apologise to me for grief,
for surely mine is worse.
Friends hesitate to talk about their loss,
for I have lost much more.
When people tell me of their fruitless search for sense,
they quickly, deprecating, add,
'Of course it's nothing when compared to yours.'

I don't want this.
I don't want bartering or weighing-scales of love.
I am not hurt by others' grief
or slighted by their rude presumption
in loving too the man I loved.
Another's tears do not deny me mine,
they all are homage
to a common cause.

For father, sister, wife or son,
what we have lost,
each one of us the same,
is him.

UNFOREWARNED

If you're grieving,
and enduring
the insistent interface with life,
it's not the big dates that defeat you,
birthdays, deathdays,
you see those coming and you build your shield,
rehearse the grief so many times within your mind,
that on the day you feel just emptiness,
not pain.

What pierce straight through
that careful primed defence
are little things,
the spindly arrows of the nondescript;
a profile glimpsed, a snatch of song,
some tiny, aching echo from another time,
which catch you quite unprepared
and bring you to your knees.

It makes you see
why execution by a thousand cuts
is so much crueller than the axe,

and leaves you fearful
of unanticipated slices
still to come.

A WALK BY MOONLIGHT

'Take me for a walk,' you said,
a sudden lucid burst of words,
a sudden powerful grab at life.

Released now by the wheelchair
from your encaged bed,
it seemed your mind had also taken wings,
and carried you,
resurgent,
back to us.

Dusk lay outside,
the dark but briefly held at bay.
Inside, only us;
your father, frail with age and worry,
you, six foot of near dead weight,
and me.

Your father's eyes met mine,
and both at once resolved,
grasping this rare small gift to bring you,
we'd take you for your walk.

The chair, the clumsy turning frame,
all the grotesque props of immobility,
were,
our muscles straining,
loaded in the car.
A short drive, then unloaded,
as were you,
a puppet, hung by half your strings.
All three of us at the extremes now of our strength.
Disaster, real hurt, just a slip away,
all to take a sick man for a walk.

In sudden silence, all the night was ours.
Descending geese still arrowed in to plough
the mirrored surface of the lake,
where swans,
great ghostly globes afloat,
glowed faint.
But then you raised your arm to point,
and there it was,
a few heartbeats away,
a heron,
stillness frozen into flesh,
darting its slicing glance into the river's depths.
We stood enthralled.

And then you grinned at us in triumph,
that you, half-blind,
had snared its beauty for us,
and in that moment
made the night complete,
as darkness, final,
drew its shawl across our sight.

I go there still,
alone now, partly.
And if, on certain evenings in the dusk,
I see a heron statued on the bank,
I smile,
or weep,
for truly these two are the same,
and in my mind I greet it,
in your name,
as I recall the late spring night
you took us,
joyous,
for a walk.

A PRESSURE LIFTED

Last night I heard a poet read his work.
He spoke of tiny auks in Iceland,
whose hunters kill them
by the gentlest pressure on their hearts.
The poet hoped that human death
might be the opposite -
a pressure softly lifted at the last.

At once I was transported to your death.
And I beside you, lips against your cheek,
whispering words of love,
and of permission.
My hand upon your chest,
your heartbeat whispered back beneath my palm.

You breathed in great and ragged inhalations
but greater still the silence,
long
and dreadful,
in between.

Then one last breath.

And in that final silence I could feel, beneath my hand,
your heartbeat falter,
flicker,
die.

To feel
in such a small cessation,
a human life go out!

I lifted clear my hand, and with the fingers
closed your eyes.

But now, just like that poet, I reflect:
which was the last sensation of your life?

Was it the gentle pressure of my hand upon your heart?
Or was it, rather,
my fingers' final, soft release?

SWIFTS

The swifts are back!
As I strode out in chilly evening light,
watching plucky duck pairs bobbing,
leaning their breasts
into the wind-whipped waves,
suddenly
there cascaded round me
a scattering stream of wheeling swifts,
as if a giant firework had exploded in the air,
to send a spray of fizzing sparks
across the water's startled face.
Spinning like glinting slate shards
struck from some unyielding cliff
they swooped and twittered in their glorious dance.

Then suddenly,
and quite unbidden,
in my mind
a memory rose,
from another night,
of just this same enchantment in the sky,
the first time we had seen the swifts' display.

I knew from the amusement on your face
what you were thinking as you gazed,
a view you'd voiced in glee before,
'You know they're doing that just for fun?
Don't tell me catching flies needs such exuberance.
That's sheer enjoyment, lucky sods!'

And for a moment, in your mind,
I hoped that you were soaring with the swifts.

What unexpected treasure I had found!
That memories of some good within that bitter time,
though buried deep,
had still survived.

Perhaps by skimming from my memory's pool
the scum of congealed pain
that clogged my brain,
I have released some lighter thoughts
to rise in gentle bubbles,
and break upon
the surface of my mind.

If so, that's twice those somersaulting swifts
have brought to tired and saddened lives,
the sweetest burst of pleasure in the brain.

CONNECTION

I wonder if the others do this,
the disconnected,
the dispossessed,
searching always for some means to
re-attach.

At first I chose to count a glimpse of heron on my walks
as a calling-card from you,
somehow fitting
in its slender elegance.

But sadly herons are quite rare.

And so I thought the swifts might speak for you as well,
as witty flicks of humour in your name.

Then, as I walked along the hedgerows,
on Fathers' Day,
I saw a poppy head,
propped, like a lipsticked grin,
on a fencepost,
a botanical Cheshire cat.

Perhaps it had been spun there by a passing cyclist,
or placed there by another walker,
sad at its beheading.

Or put there,
just to lift my heart,
by you,
knowing,
as of course you do,
my special love of poppies.

So now that's herons, swifts and poppies,
carrying your message,
your connection,
back to me
from some unlikely astral plane!

But,

        if it lifts my heart,

                and it does,

what harm?

AN EARLY NIGHT

You always used to walk so quickly,
marching from each moment
to the next.
Half-running,
breathless,
I would try to catch you
as you strode away again.

From time to time,
I gained a breather,
as you thrust a camera in my hand.
You always wanted photographs,
and I,
self-conscious,
gladly turned the lens on you.

But then,
by nightfall,
you'd start to falter,
and before I knew it
you would fall asleep,
leaving me cheated,
the night's romantic promise lost.

Now I gaze into the evening of my life,
with you already deep asleep,
exhausted
from your day's adventures,
leaving me to sit here,
in the dusk,
surrounded by a gallery of albums
to help me
see out the night.

DEVELOPMENTS

My grandfather developed
his own photographs.
And as a child I stood beside him
in the dark,
while in the amniotic slew of chemicals
he dipped the prints.

We watched the images
with ghostly summons grow,
into the paper,
there,
beneath the surface,
like the faces of the drowned.

I stand now in the dark again.

But this time,
like a film re-spooling,
the face upon the sheet is fading,
features slipping off the page,
dissolving,

Until the paper,
once more,
is
blank?

TROMPE D'OEIL

And really, I mean,
he didn't even look like you!
For a start he was an inch or two too short,
and losing his hair –
although I didn't see that
till he turned around,

but the walk was right,
and you did have a shirt a lot like that one,
once.

For the eye sees
what it's trained to see.
And you must be engraved
upon some inner lens.

Just like the *trompe d'oeil* of the pretty girl,
whose face will suddenly emerge
from that old witch's twisted shape,
you've started to leap out at me
from men I catch
a passing glimpse of.

Though,
of course,
as soon as I look closely,

I see
my mistake.

ALL I HAVE TO DO....

Finally,
I dream of you.
Not, as I'd feared,
that your death was
all some mad mistake,
that you are well
and all this anguish
itself the dream.

Instead,
a tide of tears
I weep,
through night-long hours
and wake
wrung-out,
emptied.

Worse still,
I find you in my bed
and have to tell you
sadly,
you must go.
'You're dead,'
I tell you firmly.
as you stare,
aggrieved
and disbelieving.

How cruel it seems,
that, aching for your presence
when awake,
in my dreams
I must drive you
away.

WALKING

I always hated walking;
a pointless, aimless wandering,
to nowhere much and back again.
How unforeseen it was then,
when our world turned upside down,
that we began to walk.

Perhaps to talk in privacy,
unheard by those who'd worry if they knew.
Or to carry pain away,
to leave our home a refuge.
But also, slowly, we began to find
an unexpected solace in those gentle times,
amongst the poppy fields and hedgerows,
along the quiet canal.

We found a place to take our fears,
and, briefly, let them dissipate,
into a wider space,
than our small lives could stretch to,
somehow,
to dilute them for a while.

So when, at last,
a full year on,
you came back home to me
from antiseptic wards, and sickly air,
it's no surprise we once more chose to walk,
though you of course
had wheels beneath you now,
our loving talks conducted in our minds,
not in our mouths.
But still somehow the peace was there for us.

Until, for you, came final peace at last.

Another year,
a full twelve months of grief,
the seasons swing around once more,
and, finally emerging,
I begin again to walk.
I don't pretend I went at first in hope
or that at once the place was there for me.
But, slowly,
after many tears,
and long,
again one-sided,
dialogues with you,
I find at last some ease,
some hope that,
somewhere in the future,
peace might wait.

Until it comes,
and even after, who can tell,
amid the poppy fields and hedgerows,
with you beside me in my thoughts,
I keep on walking.

KINGFISHER

Sprung from the willow bough's slack bow
a jewelled arrow shoots
clean across the pliant surface.

An iridescent sapphire spark,
struck from a fiery anvil,
his blue heat sizzles over cool canal.
Clear up the centre,
as if strung upon a wire,
he streaks.

I hold my breath,
enchanted,
till he dips a metalled wing
in irreverent salute
and vanishes.

STARTING OVER

I change my diet.
go walking,
take up archery,
lose weight, grow tanned,
and buy new clothes
in smaller sizes.

Friends smile, and wonder,
Has she found someone new?
And they're right,
I have.

It's me.

GIVING VOICE

The hardest thing
was seeing you lose your voice.
For one so eloquent,
so quick of wit,
to hear you struggle for the simplest word,
watch you start to speak,
fluent at first,
then falter in frustration
as the meaning slipped away.

To have to tell a man
who kept whole rooms in thrall
that what he now spoke
made no sense at all.
A man who revelled in that audience held,
who loved the sound of laughter he had won,
reduced to gesture
and to mute appeals.

Yet with what dignity, what grace,
you bore such bitter culling
of your sharpest skill,
and to the end,
by any means you could,
an eyebrow raised,
a telling curl of lip,
a glint of eye that never wholly died,
you showed quite clearly
that your humour
and your spirit
lived.

Even as so much was cruelly stolen from your life
you kept on giving
until life itself was gone.

How fitting, how ironic, then,
that by that very life,
and death,
you bring to me
a last, sweet, loving gift.

My voice.